Business Valuation

A Step-by-Step Beginner's Guide to Valuing a Company

Julian Ashford

ISBN: 9781807650292

Published by TPSA Publishing

Table of Content

INTRODUCTION

Whether you're looking to buy or sell a business, to invest in the stock market or become a business angel, or simply to get a better idea of what your business is worth, this book contains all the information you need.

Each type of valuation method is introduced in turn: assets based, revenue based, earnings and cash flow based, together with discounted cash flow and 'rule of thumb' valuations. We'll show you how to calculate the value of the business, but we'll also discuss the strengths and weaknesses of each method of valuation; where they're useful and where they are of limited value.

Does that sound as if the book is a dry, mathematical text? Far from it. We've given real examples throughout the book, we talk about the 'art' as well as the 'science' of valuation, and we've also included a chapter on buying or selling a business and focused on due diligence ('kicking the tyres').

Once you've read this book you should have a good handle on how to value a business. Maybe you won't be a highly paid McKinsey consultant, but you'll have what it takes to know what a business is worth, and you'll have enough smarts to avoid the obvious traps and pitfalls, such as 'dressing up' profits. That can make the difference between selling your business at a price that funds your retirement, and coming up short - or the difference between buying a great business at a good price, or paying over the odds for a moribund company.

CHAPTER 1 – WHY YOU MIGHT NEED A BUSINESS VALUATION

If you're busy running your business day to day, then the numbers you're worried about are probably sales, receivables, profit margins, and cash. You may be concerned about debt and working to reduce it, or you may be focused on increasing the utilisation of your fixed assets. What your business is worth is probably not a number you're particularly concerned about.

But business valuation becomes very, very important in certain situations. For instance, stock market analysts do nothing *but* business valuation - they're always running the numbers to see whether a company could potentially be worth more than the stock market price. Finding undervalued companies for their clients to buy is the soul of the job. But business owners and entrepreneurs might need a business valuation for all kinds of reasons.

- Takeovers - If you want to buy another business, you're going to need to have an idea of what it ought to cost before you make an approach, so you'll want to do a business valuation, even if it's sketchy one, first. Besides, you need to know whether you can afford it!
- Retirement - For many business owners, the sale of their business is crucial to providing funds for their retirement. Other entrepreneurs simply want to free funds up at some point by selling part or the whole of the business. Doing a business valuation can prevent nasty surprises - you don't want to find your business is really worth far less than you thought.
- Divorce is another life event that sometimes changes the destiny of owner-managed or family businesses. If the business is one partner's main asset, a valuation will be critical in establishing a fair settlement.
- Buying out a partner, or taking on a new one - if a partner is taking a share in the business, a valuation is crucial to making sure that the deal makes sense for both sides.

- Fund raising - Whether a fund raising is through friends and family, a venture capital firm, crowdfunding or a stock market flotation, a business valuation will be crucial to planning the financing.
- Demergers - Selling off a subsidiary business can sometimes make good business sense, either to raise money for the core operation, or to concentrate management effort, but whether it makes financial sense or not will depend on the valuation.
- Administration or insolvency proceedings always require a business valuation.
- In the case of a family business, passing the business on to a new generation can involve tax liabilities. To estimate those in advance, a business valuation is vital.
- Brand valuation is a special case - some businesses with a number of different brands decide to sell one in order to focus investment on the others.
- Legal cases occasionally turn on questions of the value of a business. For instance, a misleading advertising campaign by a competitor damaged a holiday rentals business. They employed a business valuation expert to argue for damages based on the value of the business rather than simply the cost of refunding cancellations.
- Serial entrepreneurs quite often buy a second business after selling off the old one. Experienced managers who have been made redundant use their redundancy money to buy a business. In both cases, having a good feel for business valuation can help assess what kind of business is available for a certain level of funding - or what additional financing might be needed.

More generally, you might want to think about using business valuation as a way of thinking about the creation of value in your business. Quite a lot of businesses make a living for their owners, but don't increase in value from one year to the next. Carrying out a valuation periodically can show whether your business is increasing or decreasing in value, and it's also a good way to identify assets which are not earning their keep, such as unused cash or real estate that is worth more on the property market than it is to the business.

Many business owners don't know what their business is worth - and that can lead to problems. For instance:

- Fred always thought he would be able to sell his business to fund his retirement. Because he's invested in the business, rather than putting his money into a pension fund, he needs at least $750,000 that he can invest to provide himself with an income. But when he employs a business broker, he's told the business is worth less than $500,000. If he'd done a proper valuation every year or so, he wouldn't have been caught by surprise.
- Angela runs a small chain of florists and knows that one of her competitors is up for sale. That could expand her chain considerably - but she doesn't think she can afford the price. However, a business valuation shows her that she'll be able to fund the acquisition through borrowings or, possibly, through giving the retiring owners a stake in the enlarged business.
- Bob thinks it's time for him to retire and hand on the publishing business he's built up. Unfortunately, the business is worth much more than he thinks. Unfortunately? Yes, because he and his daughter are unpleasantly surprised by the size of the potential tax bill. They need to take some speedy advice from a tax specialist.

Remember, too, that valuations can change. For instance, the valuation of technology companies changed dramatically during the tech boom and bust. Netscape was expected to list at $14 a share in 1995, but the IPO took place at $28 a share, and shares rocketed on the first day of trading to $75. It was valued at $6 billion, and yet had revenues of only $85m - seventy times *revenues*! That kicked off five years of craziness, which all came unstuck in the 2001 tech crash.

In fact, the tech crash created some great investment opportunities. As well as lossmaking, early-stage tech businesses, computer software and services companies with long established profitable operations saw their share prices hammered. Investors who picked companies up at those low valuations - and businesses which acquired competitors at knock-down prices - saw massive returns in the next couple of years as markets normalised.

Valuations can also change as a result of changing market conditions. For instance, many retailers are now seeing the value of their businesses diminish, as internet competition bites. Even if their revenues and profits aren't yet suffering, because investors expect that conditions will become more difficult, they are not willing to pay as highly for retail businesses as they once were. Remember, while valuations are based on past financial figures, they also include a judgement about what's likely to happen in the future.

There are also several different ways of valuing businesses, and the preferred valuation method can change over time. For instance, when it was first listed on the stock exchange, British Airports Authority (BAA) was treated as a services business, and valued on the basis of its earnings. However, as it invested in retail space and increased the percentage of its revenues that came from rentals to retailers, it began to be seen as a property company and valued instead on the basis of its net asset value, leading to a more than 100% increase in the share price.

Imagine a city center with numerous bars. Among them are two you've been asked to look at for a valuation. One bar has just kept on doing the same thing it has always done. It has a great reputation in the local community but its sales aren't growing - it's just moseying along. The other has completely refurbished the space, becoming a craft ale bar with a microbrewery and an attached restaurant, and has tripled its sales. Which of these businesses is worth more?

Well, that's a trick question. Because real estate values in the city are so high, no one really cares about how much money the businesses are making - they're both valued on their real estate. The value of the craft ale bar, though, is higher, because the other bar is in a historic building and there are planning restrictions on what it can be used for.

Valuation breaks down into two processes. First of all, before you can do any valuation, there's an information gathering process. For a stock market investor that might be as simple as getting a hold of the annual report or 10-K filing and looking up some comparable data on Google Finance. For a valuation of a small business that you're thinking of buying, it could include getting the financial statements from the sales agent, looking for industry comparables or 'rules of thumb', looking at local real estate values, and tracking down news items on the company in local papers or trade magazines.

The next stage is the valuation - and in the case of a discounted cash flow valuation you'll also need to make some forecasts about future performance. (If you're buying a business, that might also include the results of any management decisions you intend to take, such as closing an unprofitable part of the business, or expanding into export markets, though you should be fairly conservative in your assessment of what you can do in the short term.) While some valuers have particular preferences for one or another style of valuation, we'd advise you to carry out all of them - it's extremely useful to know what the variance is between different valuation methods.

For instance, they may all come out indicating roughly the same value, in which case, you should be fairly confident that you have the right range of valuations. Or you may find one is an outlier - for instance in the case of a loss-making tech company that's still in the development stage, a revenue based method might give you a value much higher than any of the other methods. If it's a lot higher than the discounted cash flow method, that might be an indication that the sector has gotten overheated. We'll talk more about the strengths and weaknesses of each method of valuation in the relevant chapter, and give you some real world examples of how each method can be applied.

Some books on valuation get very theoretical. Look at some of the standard texts used by accountants and business valuers and you'll see pages of equations that remind you of algebra lessons at school - but you don't need advanced maths to get a basic grasp of valuation. More, doing valuation right as a business owner or buyer is about understanding the basic structures of valuation and how they might apply to an individual business, and getting down to the nitty-gritty.

Should you use a professional valuer? Well, if you're making a big step like selling your business, using professionals always helps: you wouldn't write your own contracts (at least, we hope you wouldn't) or sign off your own accounts; you'd ask a lawyer and an auditor. But if you arrive with a good understanding of how valuations are done, you'll be doing yourself a favor:

- you'll know what information the valuer will need, so you'll have it ready,

- you'll already have an idea about the range of potential values for the business, so you're less likely to be surprised by the result of the valuation,
- and you'll be able to discuss the valuation intelligently with the valuer and ask about the assumptions that have been made, and what might change the value.

What do professionals bring to the party? Often, a business valuer will have specialised knowledge of a particular sector. That can be useful if you're thinking of buying a business in an industry you haven't worked in before. Business valuers have a wide experience of different kinds of valuation situations - for sale, for purchase, for divorce proceedings - and often, they've got a shrewd idea of how assets might be 'dressed up' for sale, or sometimes, how profits might be disguised in order to get a low valuation (for instance if an ex-wife is claiming a sum based on the earnings of the business).

Perhaps, too, professional valuers have developed a suspicious nature!

You'll also want to take advice on tax, financing, and legal issues, and business valuers - particularly if they work within an accountancy practice - can help you with up-to-date information on the rules and regulations. Good tax advice, in particular, can save you a huge amount of money and is well worth taking.

On the other hand, we reckon you should steer clear of online appraisal services. If you read through this book you'll be able to do just as a good a job. And watch out for business brokers who offer valuations; they are hardly unbiased, since they're remunerated on the sale of a business, not for their advice. Feel free to buy from one, or use one to sell - but run a double-check on any valuation they come up with.

Having a good idea what your business is worth - particularly if you've run the slide rule over the numbers every six months for a few years - can stop you from being taken to the cleaners. For instance, it'll stop you investing more in property and equipment than the business is actually worth as a going concern - every year, thousands of restauranteurs go bust having invested more in their premises than they'll ever earn back. It'll stop you from taking on a partner and giving away shares in the business at a crazily low valuation. And it can stop you wasting your wealth by paying too much for a business that isn't really all that hot.

For business owners, valuation can be a great reality check. If you use discounted cash flow to look at the returns, you can ask yourself: would you be better off investing in the business, or putting your money in the bank, or investing in real estate? You might find that if you split the business up, you'd get more than the business is worth as a whole. That happened when Racal Electronics split off its baby mobile phone business in 1991 - the 'rump' businesses were actually valued by the Stock Exchange at less than zero! Or you might find that there are assets, such as excess property, that aren't contributing to the value of the business and could be sold off or leased out.

CHAPTER 2 – THE BASIC CONCEPTS BEHIND BUSINESS VALUATION

When you carry out a business valuation, you'll be looking at a number of factors.

- You'll be looking at *estimates of future returns* - what cash flow the business is going to deliver. A really basic example - an investor buying shares in an income fund will assess the investment by looking at the yield, that is, how much he will get in dividends as a percentage of the price paid. 5% is better than 4.5% - all other things being equal.
- You'll be looking at *comparisons with other businesses or assets*. If a comparable business is rated at ten times earnings, that's a basis for assessing what yours might be worth. It might need to be adjusted up or down. Again, a really basic example is looking at houses in the same street - if one is worth $200,000, then a house with the same number of bedrooms and the same size garden further down the road is probably worth much the same, but you might need to adjust that figure if it's in a bad state of repair, or if it needs a makeover.

People sometimes say that an asset is worth 'what the market will bear'. Let's examine that a bit more closely. If you put an asset up for auction, and ensure it's well advertised, then you'll find out exactly what the market will bear - it's possible that two bidders will compete against each other to take the auction way beyond what you thought you'd get. Equally, it's possible a lowballer will be the only one to make a bid.

But where do the bidders get their idea of what to pay for the asset? They have most probably seen a similar asset for sale elsewhere, and noted the price. That's comparison - the second basis for a business valuation. Business purchasers may also have worked out what buying a new piece of equipment could save them, perhaps by cutting their fuel costs or making their manufacturing process quicker and less costly - that's looking at estimates of future returns. The bidder might not always have done the sums, but simply says, "Hey, next time I buy a vehicle for my fleet, I'll get a hybrid, because the price is 10% more but I reckon I'll save 20% on fuel". That's not awfully scientific, but it works.

'What the market will bear' may be based on a market of relatively inexpert purchasers, or of purchasers who are wised up on exactly what valuation they believe applies, but business assets - whether that's a company, or stocks and shares - always have their price set on the basis of an analysis of the prospects for the business, and the valuation of similar businesses, whether that's explicit or simply understood.

Absolute vs relative valuations

An absolute valuation model assesses the business by looking at its future earnings, dividend yield or cash flow, and assessing what they are worth in today's money. There's no comparison to other businesses - which can be useful if, as with some disruptive tech companies, there's not a valid comparison out there; the only variable in the equation is the cost of capital or discount rate that you use to calculate the valuation.

A relative valuation on the other hand compares the company you're looking at with other businesses, usually competitors or peers in the same sector - so you'd compare an IT consultant with other consultancies, a consumer goods manufacturer with other similar manufacturers.

Relative valuations can, however, be made broader. For instance, if you were buying a house to rent it out, you could compare other income-generating assets such as bonds, investment funds, or commercial property, to find out which investment would deliver the best return. Sometimes it can be useful, instead of looking at the business sector a company is in, to consider the kind of value it delivers - if it's a mature company which delivers regular dividends, it might be best compared with other companies which are similarly mature.

Factors that can affect valuation

When you're looking at a business, the valuation will generally depend on various factors. For instance, it will be affected by

- earnings - present and forecast.
- The physical assets employed in the business - what are they worth?

- Revenues - sometimes you'll look at sales value, because the company isn't profitable, or has low profitability for some reason.
- Intangible assets such as proprietary technology, goodwill, or brands.

Many valuations are forward-looking - they are based on expectations of future benefits to come from owning the business. Even if your forecasts are a bit back-of-envelope, making an effort to predict future revenues and cash flows is always worthwhile.

The forward-looking nature of valuations explains why stock markets sometimes move rapidly in response to a missed earnings number. The market isn't just reacting to the shortfall - it's also downgrading its expectations of future earnings. That's one reason why when Intel downgraded its earnings advice by 2-4% in 2000 the shares fell 30%.

Think about it this way. You expected to get $100 this year. You expected that return to grow by 10% a year, so you'd get $110, $121, $133, then $146. Now, this year's return is cut to $96. You're $4 down, right?

Well, if you're looking forwards, you'd expect future returns to be lower, too, as you're starting from a lower base. So just assuming you'll still get 10% growth, but starting from $96 rather than $100, you'd get future returns of $105, $116, $127 and $140 - so over the whole period, you'd be $24 worse off. That's a more significant fall in the value of the business than the 4% downgrade made it appear.

That's rather a simplistic example but it gives you an idea of how a downgrade of this year's earnings can affect future expectations. In the case of Intel, the effect was particularly savage, and you could argue that since this downgrade came right at the top of the tech boom, the shares were also overvalued. Investors had drastically overestimated the growth rate of companies like Intel and IBM. (Markets tend to work rather like a piece of elastic - you can stretch it and stretch it, for ever such a long time, but eventually it will snap back violently.)

Sometimes, the value to different buyers can be different. This is often seen when a business that's quoted on the stock exchange is acquired by a competitor or by a corporate raider - the value of the shares can increase dramatically. Stock exchange investors are buying a financial asset, and they can't do anything to change its value; they only own a small percentage of the shares. A corporate buyer, on the other hand, who takes 100% ownership, will be able to change the business's strategy, can probably cut duplicate costs, and will gain synergies that make the acquisition more valuable.

'Marriage value' is a concept from the real estate sector that describes the extra value that comes from combining the freehold and leasehold interests in a given property. It's a nice phrase that describes how putting two businesses together can be worth more than the sum of the parts.

Quality of earnings

As well as considering the basic numbers, you'll also want to think about the *quality* of the business and its earnings. This includes factors such as

- 'Moats' - This is what Warren Buffett calls sources of business differentiation that can keep returns high. For instance, a company might have patent protection for some of its products, or it may have a brand image other companies can't compete with (think Coca-Cola). A company with a good 'moat' has a better quality of earnings (that is, its earnings should be more sustainable) than its competitors.
- Scalability - whether the business can grow without increasing its fixed costs. For instance, eBay is scalable, because it costs nothing to add another customer. Webvan, on the other hand, wasn't scalable, because although it was an internet retailer, it did its own delivery - every 500 or so new customers, it had to buy another delivery van. EBay is a huge business now - and Webvan went bust.
- Cyclicality. Some industries tend to work in cycles. That's the case with heavily capital intensive sectors such as mining or chemicals; often (not always) it's driven by commodity prices. When things are going well, everyone invests in new plant. But the new plant isn't profitable at once, because it's only working at a small percentage of capacity, so earnings fall. And if all the businesses in the sector have new plant coming onstream at the same time, the effect is even worse. Earnings fall, and the business valuation falls - until,

gradually, the plant fills up (sometimes because revenues grow, and sometimes because one or two competitors give up and leave the sector). Cyclical earnings are relatively low quality, and timing can be a big factor in making a successful purchase or sale.

Valuation isn't just about numbers. Although a lot of this book is about teaching the basic mathematical equations for valuing a business, any valuation needs to be informed by an understanding of the business and the conditions in which it operates. So you'll need to look at corporate strategy. Is a business a price maker or a price taker - does it sell its products at a premium, or accept prices set by leaders in its sector? Is it an innovator, or does it have 'me-too' products? How do its costs compare with competitors? The answers to these questions will tell you whether you want to pay a full price for a great company, or look for a bargain price for a business that has a few problems.

You'll want to look at trends over time. With retail businesses the gross margin (sales less cost of sales, as a percentage of total sales) can tell you how well the company is doing. If the gross margin is shrinking, that might be due to greater competition, or cost inputs might be going up (for instance if the retailer imports its stock and the currency has moved against it) and the business isn't able to pass that cost on to the consumer. With services business and manufacturing you'll want to look at the pre-interest profit margin (ebit / sales).

Make sure, if you're valuing a business in an industry you don't know well, to take a look at the general background trends.

- Is the industry growing or shrinking? Is it consolidating? Acquiring smaller businesses in an industry that's consolidating can be a way to gain greater purchasing power and clean up - but it can also be relatively high risk.

- Are there any disruptive technologies that compete with the business you're looking at? They can quickly kill the preceding generation. In 1984, Kodak was by far the leader in the US photographic market. In the 1990s, though, it was slow to launch a digital camera; it got the market wrong, seeing digital cameras as expensive luxuries rather than commodities, and so its cameras were over-specified and made at too high a cost. By 2012, it had to file for bankruptcy. Right now, the automotive industry looks at risk

- electric cars, self-driving cars, and hybrids represent a huge investment on which car firms are mostly making very little money.

- Is the basis of sales changing? From 2000 onwards many software companies moved from selling one-time software licences to selling subscriptions (Software as a Service, or SaaS). For many of them, that's been a really good deal - but they suffered several years of earnings disruption as instead of selling $50,000 a licence, they were only making $15,000 or so a year in subscriptions on the same client.
- Is regulation tightening up? When government starts taking notice of what has generally been an unregulated industry, that can increase costs and even put some firms out of business.

Understanding the business will help you work out the price you want to pay, but it will also help you select the best model for forecasting value. In a mature industry, yield and earnings are good bases for a valuation - in a growth industry yield is much less important and you'd probably want to look at discounted cash flow.

Adjusting the numbers

Preparing a good valuation means looking further than the headline numbers. You'll probably want to adjust the numbers found in the financial statements in several ways, using figures in the notes to the accounts.

For instance, you'll want to remove non-recurring income from the figures. Suppose the business you're looking at made a gain on the sale of some properties last year; if it's a printer, and not normally involved in real estate, then you'll want to take that out of the earnings numbers, because you can't expect it to recur. On the other hand, if a business has had the bad fortune to have a flood that wiped out half its inventories, you might want to adjust the earnings and revenues up - the flood-hit earnings number doesn't represent the true profit-making potential of the business.

You'll also possibly want to exclude non-operating assets - assets owned by the business but which don't play a part in generating profits, or which are non-core. For instance, a manufacturing business that owns a building it doesn't use, perhaps because it downsized its operations some time ago, or a downtown retail outlet that owns and rents out a flat above the shop. (In the second example, you'd also need to exclude the earnings from that rental from the profit and loss account.)

Accountants who prepare and audit financial statements have all kinds of rules for what is and isn't non-recurring. You can ignore them. If you're buying a business, it's your call what you regard as non-recurring or non-operating, because at the end of the day it's your money on the line. If you're selling, you might need to take a bit more notice of what your accountant says.

You may want to check the business owner's personal benefits and bonuses. Club memberships, entertainment, insurance, and a nice car, unless you are quite sure that the CEO of a similarly sized stock market quoted business would get exactly the same, subtract them from the costs of the business. It's often tax efficient for the business owner to source benefits through the business rather than personally - but that's a personal decision, not a business decision. To get to the true profitability of the business, which ill let you establish its true value, you need to rewind the accounts.

Going concern vs liquidation value

A business that is operating, and making profits, or is likely to make them in future, sells on the basis of those profits. It's a going concern and it's valued in the expectation that it will continue in business and carry on making profits.

On the other hand, sometimes a business is staring extinction in the face. A company that still has only analogue products that are being replaced by digital services isn't going to last long. That doesn't mean it's worth nothing. But you wouldn't value it on the going concern basis. Instead, you'd look at what the different assets are worth if it's broken up and everything is sold off. That's its liquidation value.

It's possible to do well by finding companies where the liquidation value exceeds the price being asked. For instance, where real estate assets in sought-after areas are not being well utilised by a failing retailer, there may be value in acquiring the business only to close it down. However, taxation aspects need to be considered in advance or such a deal can come badly unstuck. Equally, if a business is being sold at liquidation value but you think you can fix the ongoing business model, you may get a bargain. In this book, though, we're concentrating on valuing businesses as a going concern.

Choosing the right model

Choosing the right valuation model is important. There are two factors that will generally affect your decision.

1. The availability and quality of data to support the model. For instance, if a business isn't making profits yet, obviously an earnings-based model isn't going to be helpful. (In the case of some businesses which are currently loss making, but where management action could turn them around, you might be able to base an earnings related valuation on a forecast, but it would need to be a robust one - for instance, if closing the ten percent most unprofitable product lines down would enable the business to turn a profit.) You may not have detailed data on cash flow or forecast earnings; using a valuation based on historic data is the best you can do.
2. The appropriateness of the model to the business. For instance, discounted cash flow analysis is most helpful for early-stage businesses, and for capital intensive businesses which have invested heavily in new facilities. A mature business might be more suited to dividend yield and price-earnings based valuations. We'll discuss this more with regard to each type of valuation in the relevant chapter.

The importance of record keeping

Meticulous record keeping is important when you're valuing a business. Even if you're just doing back-of-envelope numbers, keep a file copy that specifies all the following data:

the date of the valuation,

why you made the valuation

any assumptions made (for instance, growth rates)

the calculations

the comparisons used (eg. listed companies, with the relevant share price)

the sources of data

GDP growth, interest rates, the level of the Dow Jones or FTSE index, and relevant commodity prices or key industry data at the time you made the valuation.

Economic conditions can change, as can stock market indices - keeping this data logged means you can look at a past valuation and immediately see whether it's still up with events, or whether you need to run the numbers again to take account of the changes.

CHAPTER 3 – PROFIT BASED APPROACHES

Profit based approaches are simple to use and remain the most commonly quoted ratios used for valuing shares on the stock markets. They can be applied to historic data, or more usefully, to forecasts. In each case, you'll need to identify comparable quoted companies, as these are relative valuations which depend on comparisons.

Dividend yield

At a really simple level we can say that investors are interested in what a company distributes to them in dividends - their tangible reward for investing. That comes out of its profits, once all the costs of the business (including tax) have been paid. In essence, it's similar to the interest on a bank account or the coupon on a bond. Calculating the yield ratio relates the absolute level of the dividend paid to the price of the share.

Yield % = dividend / share price x 100

It's an easy figure to calculate and, for individuals who want to invest in shares in order to build an annual income, it's a really useful ratio. However, it's not all that useful in business valuation, for several reasons:

- Many smaller business reward their owners in different ways, for instance with business perks or loans, or simply the ability to draw on capital, rather than paying dividends;
- Dividends aren't a good proxy for profit. A company might decide not to pay any dividends at all, but to retain and reinvest all the money; or it might pay out half its post-tax profit out as dividends; or it might even pay out all its profits (REITs are actually obliged to do this). If you took three companies that made the same profit, but made those three different decisions on distribution to shareholders, you'd have one valued at nil - and of the other two, one would be worth twice the value of the other. That's obviously not correct!
- Most companies that pay a high percentage of their profits out to investors do so because reinvesting their funds in the business wouldn't generate an adequate return. They are mature businesses,

with relatively predictable earnings and dividends. On the other hand, businesses that are growing fast and making good returns are more likely to keep money back for investment.

Dividend yield can sometimes provide a check on other ratios, though, so while we wouldn't tell you it's the right way to value companies, it's still worth calculating it if you have the right data. But the ratios we really want to look at relate to the profits of the business - what's *available* to distribute to shareholders, if you like, before the company takes a decision on whether to pay a dividend or how much it should be.

Price Earnings Ratio

This is another stock market classic that all investors will look at. It's on the front page of almost all analysts' research and it's the gold standard of quoted company valuation. It has the advantage of being very simple to work out. Effectively you're looking at the post tax profit per share compared to the share price;

PER = Share price / Earnings per share, or at total company level

PER = Market capitalisation / Post-tax profit

If the company paid out 100 percent of its post-tax profit as dividends, the PER tells you how many years you'd have to wait till your initial investment was paid back. (You can also calculate an *earnings yield*, which uses the same figures but is calculated like the dividend yield, as EPS / Share price x 100 - that's intriguing, as you can compare it with other investments such as bonds or real estate, but it's rarely used as a valuation technique.) Another way of looking at the PER is that it shows how much investors are willing to pay for each dollar of earnings.

Using the PER properly requires finding quoted company comparators. You'll usually be looking at companies in the same sector, but sometimes there aren't many. In order to get a really good basis for comparison, you'll need to assess at least five or six peers, to get both mean and median values, so that you can exclude outliers such as companies that are highly valued because of takeover rumours or because they own prime real estate.

Data on public companies can be found on sites such as Google Finance, or on the S&P Dow Jones website. Often, this data will include the consensus of analysts' forecasts for the next two or three years. These will give you the basis for a rough valuation. However, it's worth reading through the news and also taking a look at the companies' accounts, and particularly the notes to the accounts, to see if there are any special factors affecting the valuation, and ensure that you're looking at an adjusted earnings number that strips out non-recurring items.

Suppose you can't find relevant comparators? That can happen. For instance, in the UK, real estate agents were very rarely listed until the end of the 1990s; it was only once the sector began to consolidate that companies such as Foxtons, Winkworth, and LSL joined the market. If you can't find direct comparisons you have several alternatives available:

- Use the PER of a relevant stock market index such as the Dow Jones Industrial Average or FTSE 100. But pick your index carefully! If you're looking at a technology company the NASDAQ Composite will be more appropriate. There are a range of smaller company and industry indices which might also be more appropriate to the business you're looking at than the main market index.
- Look for companies which, while not in exactly the same sector, have similar earnings profiles. For instance, if you're looking at a business that rents out portable WCs and showers for building sites and music festivals, you might look at other B2B asset rental businesses that offer trucks, tools, or construction equipment. Not quite the same business, but with the same kind of cash flow - buying big-ticket items upfront and then making a return on the investment through rental. You might not find many architects' firms on the stock exchange, but you can probably compare them to engineering consultancies or other professional services firms.

While it's possible to look at only one year's PERs, it's better to look at a range of at least two years back and two years forwards, if you have adequate data. That helps iron out divergences in performance in the short term and concentrate on long term value.

You then need to think about how the business you're valuing compares with the other companies in the analysis. Is it growing faster, or more slowly? How much smaller is it than the comparisons? You may decide, say, that a company that's growing fast and rapidly gaining market share is worth pretty much the same multiple as quoted competitors, despite the discount you'd usually give a smaller rival; whereas one that clearly has lagged in terms of its earnings growth would deserve a discount. So if the average PER for the sector is 18x, you'd only be willing to pay 70% of that for a lower quality business - that would put it on a PER of 12.6.

However, while PER is far and away the most common valuation ratio employed, it has its failings. It's post-tax and post-interest. So companies which have a large amount of debt to service will look less valuable than those which are mainly equity funded, although their business performance is otherwise very similar. It also includes depreciation and amortisation on the business's assets - that's an item that can vary widely between businesses, sometimes just because their accountants are more or less conservative than most, and it doesn't represent cash going out of the business.

To iron out those wrinkles we'll want to look at EBITDA - earnings before interest, tax, depreciation and amortisation.

Price/EBITDA and EV/EBITDA

EBITDA gives a better idea than EPS of a business's potential for generating cash, because it excludes two chunky non-cash cost items from the equation. Because it ignores interest, it also improves comparability of highly leveraged and less leveraged or cash-rich businesses. You're looking at what the business makes, irrespective of whether it's been funded by debt finance or through equity.

EBITDA has a particular advantage with early stage companies. Many will make positive EBITDA several years before they become profitable on a post-tax basis, so that you'll be able to make an EBITDA valuation long before the company can declare positive earnings per share.

The calculation of price to EBITDA is the same as for the PER: share price / EBITDA per share, or market capitalisation / EBITDA.

We can go a step further and use enterprise value rather than the market capitalisation of the shares to evaluate a business. Enterprise value looks at a firm as the sum of its equity value, together with debt - adding together all the sources of finance, not just the shares, and then subtracting the value of cash held by the company. Like EBITDA, EV removes the way the company is funded from the valuation. If you take over a business, after all, you might decide to pay off the debt, or you might decide, if there are real estate mortgages that provide good collateral, to borrow cheaply against them in order to fund investment in the business. By using EV rather than market capitalisation, you're taking assumptions about the way the business is funded out of the equation.

EV = Equity market capitalisation + borrowings - cash

Finally, you might choose to look at free cash flow (FCF) as a method of valuation. EBITDA can sometimes be misleading; when a company is investing much more in fixed assets than it is writing off in depreciation, EBITDA will flatter the 'real' performance as the company has huge amounts of cash going out of the business that aren't reflected in EBITDA. For instance, cable TV companies in the 1990s were sometimes overvalued on an EBITDA basis, because the valuation didn't include huge amounts of investment in customer acquisition that was capitalised, as well as big swathes of investment in the networks. FCF also picks up changes in working capital - for instance, if a business has to extend credit to a major customer on a big contract, or to win an export order, the cash that's being used will be subtracted from EBITDA to get to free cash flow.

FCF = EBITDA - change in working capital - capital expenditure

change in working capital = increase in receivables + increase in inventory - increase in payables

Let's run through a basic earnings related valuation. You're looking at a multiple retailer selling furnishings and accessories. So, first of all, find your comparisons and calculate the various ratios for each of them.

You might want to look at Stanley Furniture, La-Z boy, or American Woodmark. But actually, they're not very good comparisons, because although they supply the home décor market so the big trends affecting their revenues are the same, they are also manufacturers, so their margins and cash flow characteristics are different. Instead, let's look at Bed Bath & Beyond (BBBY), Kirkland (KIRK) and Pier 1 (PIR). We're also going to look at an industry sector average, Zacks Retail Home Furnishings, and the S&P 500 major stock market index.

	PER (trailing twelve months)	EV/EBITDA
BBBY	5.83	3.4
PIR	11.84	3.74
KIRK	30.15	2.09
Zacks - Retail home furnishings	16.1	-
S&P 500	21.6	-

As you can see there are some big differences between the PE ratios. One reason is that BBBY, the lowest valued company, has seen three years of its margins getting squeezed; investors are afraid it will continue to experience earnings downgrades. There's not a really clear-cut comparison for the company we're valuing; probably the Zacks estimate is the best we can get - and look, it's below the market average (the S&P 500) which tells you investors think furniture retailing is not the best quality business.

When you look at EV to EBITDA, though, there seems to be less variance, and it's interesting that the *highest* rated company on a PER basis, Kirkland's, is the *lowest* on EV/EBITDA. (It has no debt, so its EV is the same as its market capitalisation. BBBY, on the other hand, has USD 1.6bn of debt on its books, which makes its EV much larger than its USD 3bn market capitalisation.)

So now, let's take the business you're looking at. Suppose it made $70,000 post-tax last year, then you'd value it at this figure multiplied by the Zacks multiple - 16.1 x 70,000 = $1,127,000. That looks rather high and perhaps it's affected by that one very high multiple, so you might also want to look at the median valuation at 11.4 times earnings; that would only give a valuation of $798,000.

Then you add back depreciation of $40,000, interest of $32,000 and tax paid of $23,000. That gives you EBITDA of $165,000. Let's say, looking at the multiples of the comparison companies, you pick 3.4 times as the multiple, the enterprise value of the business is $527,000. The enterprise value includes $150,000 of debt, so then the equity in the business would only be worth $377,000 - a long way off the numbers generated by the PER valuation. So you'll need to make a decision on which valuation is more likely to be correct. That will require taking a good look at the comparison companies' financial statements and businesses, and perhaps using some of the other valuation methods as a check on the PER and EV/EBITDA. You'll also need to think further about whether the company you're looking at deserves more of a discount to quoted comparisons, since it's much smaller, and unquoted.

As you can see, the math is simple - but the judgments involved can sometimes be difficult!

CHAPTER 4 – REVENUES BASED APPROACHES

Sometimes we might want to value a business by considering its revenues rather than profits. Normally, of course, you're in business to make a profit, but sometimes exceptional factors might depress profitability. In that case, revenues can indicate the profit *potential* of the business. There are several kinds of situations where you might want to use a revenues based approach;

- where you think the company could increase margins by changing the pricing or mix or its products,
- where margins could be increased by cost cutting,
- where the business could be merged with another, to gain synergy benefits that will increase the margins - for instance, if you already have a complementary business,
- where a big investment in infrastructure, for instance building a telecoms network or a large production facility, means the company won't make profits till it's started to get decent utilisation on that capacity,
- or where the business is early stage, and revenues are growing fast enough that you expect it to cover its fixed costs within a few years.

Currently, price to sales is the commonest method of valuing SaaS (software as a service) companies. Earnings can remain negative for years since the company has to create the software and keep the servers running, but only gets its money back through subscriptions over a four or five year period. Revenues, therefore, give a robust method of valuing the companies on publicly available data. (A discounted cash flow forecast would be better, but companies don't give out the data that would let you make such a forecast reliably.)

There's one big advantage to revenues based approaches - the data is very, very easy to get. Whereas for free cash flow you'll usually have to calculate the number yourself, the revenue figure is the first one you'll find on any financial stats page. And the basic calculation is very, very easy.

Price to sales = Market capitalisation / total revenues

You might also want to think about using EV/sales as a valuation method where companies have very different methods of financing.

However, there are a few cases where you do have to watch out to make sure the revenue figure is comparable. Companies that charge commission, or that are franchises, sometimes have different revenue recognition policies that can make their financial statements look very different. Some software companies try to recognise revenue at an early stage of the sale and if they're too aggressive, run the risk of having to unwind the reported revenue if, for instance, the customer doesn't proceed with the second phase of a project. You also need to look carefully at sales recognition policy for companies which typically operate on the basis of long term contracts for which stage payments are made; how much revenue do they recognise, and when?

Generally, we wouldn't advise using price/sales as a lead valuation method, but it can be useful as a quick and easy way to value unprofitable companies. For instance, you might use it to perform a 'triage' on a number of prospective acquisitions, and rule out the ones that look too highly valued, before carrying out further analysis such as DCF valuation on the others.

CHAPTER 5 – ASSET BASED APPROACHES

Sometimes you'll want to take an asset based approach to valuating a business - looking at what it owns, whether that's a load of real estate, plantations, or a gold mine. But there are quite a few things to think about when you do this, because the value of the assets in the financial accounts of the business is unlikely to be very helpful.

That's because it's based on historic values - what the assets were bought for, or the cost of making them. In the case of a shop, for instance, the property might have been bought twenty years ago, and real estate prices have dramatically increased since then. Every year, the business writes off some of its investment in its assets as depreciation - suppose the shop was refurbished fully four years ago, and its accountants tell the business it should write off fittings and fixtures over five years, then all those parts of the refurbishment will be in the books at only 20% of what they cost. If they're stylish, in good condition, and relatively classic, they're probably worth significantly more than that; if they're looking grubby and outdated, they might be worth nothing at all. In either case, the book value isn't a good guide.

So we're also going to look at other ways of assessing asset values, either by adjusting the book value figure, or by looking at the assets themselves.

None the less, the basic price to book value figure is simple to calculate and can sometimes be useful. Because it usually understates the value of the assets, if you can buy a business for less than its book value, you'll probably do well. It's probably the most conservative valuation figure you can use, so it's sometimes useful for identifying bargains.

Working out price to book is very simple. Simply take the figure for shareholders' funds (that is, shares in issue plus retained profit, less minorities) and divide the share price by book value. If you get a value of less than one, you're in the money! This is particularly useful in mature, capital-intensive industries. However, price to book won't tell you whether you'll make a good return on your investment.

Back in the late 1990s, everyone thought real ale was going to die, and only the big lager breweries would survive. Canny contrarian investors and corporate acquirers looked at the fact that you could acquire some breweries for half their book value - a clear indicator that the market had gotten something wrong. A huge wave of consolidation soon got started, with Wolverhampton & Dudley breweries acquiring a number of smaller competitors after itself fighting off a takeover bid. The clue had been there in the accounts - but only the brave few investors who had done their homework made big money out of the situation.

Price to book is also a great way to give yourself a bottom marker for a valuation - it's almost always the lowest valuation of a business and with the exception of obsolete or very poorly maintained assets, you can feel pretty safe that if you pay price to book or not much more, you're not running much of a risk. As a business *seller*, you really want to stick out for more!

It can be useful to create an adjusted book value. There are various ways of doing this. Inevitably, you may end up with a bit of double counting, because individual assets are rarely specified in the accounts - it's only if you're already considering a purchase, and able to access the full financial records of the business as part of due diligence, that you'll see the individual records.

You may want to try to separate out:

- real estate - Retail, office and warehousing space can be readily compared to other properties in the area using a basic price per square metre. Industrial space is rather more difficult to value.
- Fleet - Cars, trucks, vans can all be valued using guides such as the Kelley Blue Book or used car price guides like those at autotrader.com or nadaguides.com.
- Some sector- Specific assets have known standard prices, for instance any brewer can tell you the range of prices that's usual for a given barrel-length brewery, complete, or for particular items of kit such as mash tuns or fermenters.
- Extractive industries have specific ways of valuing such assets as quarries, oil fields and wells, and mines.

In some sectors, businesses often sell on the real estate value. For instance, smaller bars and hotels are often sold on the basis of the real estate rather than business earnings. That's particularly true of B&Bs which have fewer than 10 bedrooms, and are generally valued as if they were owner-occupied homes.

Even if you're depending on the book value as declared in the financial statements you need to take a look at the assets involved. Are they well maintained and managed? You might want to think about the age of assets against industry averages. For instance, US airlines generally have fleet that's an average 12 years old. If most of the planes are older than that, not only will they be worth less, they will probably be more costly to run as they are less energy-efficient, besides offering less comfort to passengers. Office computers which are still running Windows 3.2, or which have less than 1 Gb of RAM, are probably of no value at all - they won't support up to date software and can't be upgraded, and they certainly don't have a market value.

Ridiculous assets

Buying businesses in former Eastern Europe in the 1990s was something of a gamble. Stock market rules and property ownership laws were still being drafted, businesses were competing for the first time (not always very successfully) with western imports, and appraising assets was, to say the least, interesting. What do *you* think these assets might be worth?

- One brewery had a 100-year-old German made maltings, which was still operating with two hours' maintenance a month. Its twenty-year old Soviet produced bottling plant, on the other hand, was down for at least two days a month owing to maintenance problems.

- One bakery had a machine in its production line which had been installed by Lenin (Lenin died in 1924.) It was still cranking out buns at a rate of knots, but it hadn't been cleaned since World War Two judging by the amount of oil and grease on the moving parts.

- A meat factory had a relatively new conveyor line. However, at one point, the line carrying carcasses and the line carrying the cleaned and ready for sale meat crossed each other. That was a problem - it wouldn't pass the new EU food regulations that were being introduced, and the whole factory would need to be rebuilt.

- Another food producer had just installed a completely a new machine that made perfect hamburger buns. Unfortunately, they didn't get either McDonalds or Burger King to sign up and the gleaming steel monster stood completely unused in splendid isolation, while the other production lines were running at full tilt.

CHAPTER 6 – DISCOUNTED CASH FLOW

So far we've looked mainly at relative valuations. But a discounted cash flow analysis gives you an absolute value for the business you're looking at - although, admittedly, that does depend on various assumptions that you need to feed into the model before you begin.

With a discounted cash flow, essentially you're looking at all the future income that you expect to receive from the business, and what that's worth right now. It depends on the time value of money.

You'll instinctively have a sense of the time value of money if you think about the difference between a friend who borrows five bucks and says they'll pay you back tomorrow, and the friend who borrows five bucks and doesn't get round to paying you back for months. That's simply an annoyance, of course, but it illustrates the point!

Now, if you invest $10,000 in a bank, you're going to get a return, say 5% on your funds, over the next year. So at the end of the year, your money is worth $10,500. Another way of looking at that would be to say that $10,500 in a year's time is worth $10,000 now. That's the way discounted cash flow works - it looks at what your future returns are worth in today's money. We call that the Net Present Value (NPV).

Forecasting

First of all you need to forecast the business's free cash flow. Depending on the purpose for which you're carrying out the valuation, and the information available, that could be as basic as assuming a 5% growth rate every year, or it could be a fully detailed forecast of different lines of business, with margin expansion, step changes in fixed costs and capital expenditure, and detailed working capital budgets. Obviously, if you're doing a quick valuation to work out whether it's worth asking for detailed accounts, your forecasting will be more generic, and if you're trying to finalise the valuation for a business that you've already started negotiating with, it will be more detailed and specific.

For a business that's capital intensive, you may need to build in assumptions about capacity utilisation - for instance, a hotel may not achieve high occupancy in its first year's trading, and a chemicals plant or semiconductor manufacturer might take longer to ramp up. You might also need to work out the phasing of long term projects, for instance windfarms which can take several years to build out.

Getting the forecasts right is absolutely crucial. 'GIGO' applies - garbage in, garbage out; if your assumptions aren't robust, your valuation will not be credible. Note all your assumptions, and check them against other available data. For instance, if you're assuming that the business will gain market share, how, and from which competitors? If you're assuming sales will increase, can the current fixed costs support the new level of business or will additional costs be incurred? If you're looking at a business with very rapid growth, at what point will it begin to taper off? Making an over-optimistic forecast stacks the cards against you. That's one reason the tech bubble became so overdone, because analysts were forecasting massive growth rates for all the companies in the sector, which sometimes resulted in year 5 forecasts of revenue for the various companies adding up to far more than the available market.

The discount rate

The next step in the DCF valuation model is setting the discount rate. There are various ways of doing this:

1. starting from the risk-free rate of return, and adding a risk premium,
2. using your own required rate of return,
3. using a business's weighted average cost of capital (WACC).

Calculating WACC is quite complex, and normally it's most useful for reasonably large companies with both equity and debt funding calculating the net present value of big investments. The second method can be useful, particularly for assessing stock market investments, but because you've chosen a particular rate of return, there's a bias built into it. Probably the most sensible thing to do is to use the first method.

The risk-free rate of return used is usually government bonds. With a government bond from an investment-grade issuer, you're going to get your coupons - the government won't default, so there is no risk of your not being paid. Let's say US ten year bonds pay 2.4%, that's a good place to start - though currently, interest rates are pretty low; over the century from 1900 to 2000, average rates were around 5 to 5 1/2 % in the US, 4-5% in the UK, and slightly higher in Europe.

Now you need to look at the risk of the business and what payment is required to compensate that risk. Followers of horse racing do it all the time: the odds on a horse reflect its likely performance and the risk of backing it. For instance, a horse that's always won on rock hard ground will see its odds lengthen if it rains, reflecting the risk that it might not run well on a muddy track. So you need to think about various risks that need adjustment:

- adjusting for industry risk - for instance, an industry facing disruption or rapid change is higher risk than one growing in a stable way
- adjusting for the company's stage of growth - if it's a start-up, the risk is higher
- adjusting for the size of the business - smaller companies are generally riskier.

As an example, HICL Infrastructure Company Limited, which engages in government-backed, long-term investment projects and receives inflation-adjusted payments - a pretty low risk business model - used a discount rate of 7.4% to value its projects in 2017. That represents a 5.6% risk premium over the 1.8% risk free rate based on long term government bond yields. That suggests a small company in a riskier business would need to have a considerably higher discount rate applied.

A good recourse if you're trying to set the discount rate is to see if you can find analysts' research from major investment banks or stockbrokers that uses DCF analysis to value stocks in the sector. A number of online sources also give cost of capital for various sectors - another way of getting a feel for the kind of figure that might be appropriate. (We've given a few links in the resources section at the end of this book.)

Calculating the NPV

Once you have your forecasts and your discount rate, you're ready to do the calculation. This used to be time for getting out a nice big electronic calculator and using equations; now, it's far easier to use a spreadsheet. Basically you'll want to set out the years across the top, plug in the cash flows, and then work out the discount for each year.

The basic formula is:

NPV = cash flow / discount rate, and

discount rate = $(1 + \text{interest rate})^n$,

where *n* equals the number of years before the cash flow is received. So for instance, with a 10% interest rate, in year ten, the cash flow has to be divided by $(1 + 0.1)^{10}$, or 2.59. It's easiest to work out the NPV of each year's cash flow under that year, then total the row Rather than try to build a single formula to do it, this will also let you see if any of your calculations have gone wrong, perhaps because you missed out a decimal point.

Terminal value

Suppose you've added together ten years of cash flows from the business. When you get to year ten, you still have a business left, and it will be worth something (unless you've run it into the ground). So you need to allow something for what it will be worth at that point - the terminal value. There are quite a few ways to do this.

- One is to use one of the other valuation methods, like PER or EV/EBITDA, to work out what the business will be worth at the end of the period. Then you need to discount that value back to today's money. If you sold the business at the end of the period, you'd get that value for it.
- But you might keep the business. In that case you'd be looking at another ten years' cash flows... without forecasting all those extra years individually, you can make an assumption about future growth. You might plump for constant low growth forever - a good way to forecast for companies in mature sectors that are expected to have stable growth. We show the equation for that below.
- Some models also assume a slow tapering off of growth. However, this is tricky to model mathematically. You're better off extending

the forecast period by a few years if you think high growth will continue for some time.

TV = (FCF x 1+g) / (WACC - g)

where g = the perpetual growth rate.

Remember when you're forecasting a perpetual growth rate that it's really pretty aggressive to expect a company to grow faster than the economy or the major stock market indices for ever. You're better off assuming half or three-quarters the long term GDP growth rate, for instance.

You should also think about the PER or EBITDA based terminal value in terms of what the business will look like at the end of the period. It might be growing fast now, but will it still be a high growth company, or will it be valued more like a mature business - on a lower rating? If you calculate both values, you can use them as a check on each other. Your PER based terminal value might come out with a much higher value, so then work out what value of g (perpetual growth rate) you'd need to match that value. If the company would have to grow at 10% a year in perpetuity, your PER valuation is wrong.

Once you have the terminal value, you need to discount it back to today's value, using the same discount rate as for your final year's cash flow. Add together the terminal value and the series of annual cash flows and you have your net present value - the valuation of the business at today's date.

Advantages and disadvantages of the DCF model

The discounted cash flow model has some great advantages. It's particularly good for looking at businesses that are growing rapidly, and that aren't yet profit-making but are expected to break through into profit in the medium term. That's why DCF is often used for tech companies, as well as for big capital projects. Unlike the PER or EV/EBITDA which only capture a single year's data, it values a company by looking at the sum total of its forecast cash flows for a number of years.

But it also has some major disadvantages.

- The assumptions underlying the model need to be robust. You're looking quite a long way into the future, and that is difficult to predict with any degree of certainty.

- Terminal value can affect the value markedly. As a rule, if the terminal value accounts for more than 70% of the value, you should be worried.
- A change in short term performance expectations can change the longer term prospects for the company, and the NPV, very markedly. This model is much more sensitive to short term earnings downgrades, for instance, than a comparative valuation.

A few more thoughts about cash flow

In the chapter on asset based valuations we talked about how to assess assets. That's also something you'll need to think about with regard to cash flow forecasts. If a business's assets look tired and need investment, that doesn't just affect the asset value - it also means that you'll need to invest in the business, so the capital expenditure forecasts in the DCF valuation need to reflect that. Consequently, the net present value of the company will be reduced to account for the higher capital spending.

On the other hand, if a business has been investing in its future, depressing cash flow for the past couple of years because of the high spend on new equipment, that will also need to be reflected in the forecasts, For instance a brewery that has invested in a new bottling plant will be able to cut costs as well as increasing its capacity, and that will be reflected in forecasts. Revenues should increase, and margins should also improve in future years. Since DCF looks *forwards,* that will imply a higher value for the business than valuations that are based on historic figures.

CHAPTER 7 – SECTOR-SPECIFIC APPROACHES

Valuations based on business metrics

In some business areas, you'll find that additional bases of valuation are available which reflect the nature of the business. For instance, in the hospitality sector you'll find that the price per hotel room is often quoted; that's sensible, because it's the rooms available which are the resource responsible for creating profit, with room rate and occupancy as the key drivers of profitability for the business. Language schools might be valued per student enrolled, and telecoms per subscriber - you get the idea.

These types of valuation are often the easiest to make. You don't need to spend time adjusting profits or calculating ratios.

On the other hand, a disadvantage of using this style of valuation is that it doesn't relate at all to the financial performance of the business. Two hotels might have the same number of rooms - but if one has tired décor, no marketing budget, and a location that's the wrong side of town for the business district, it could be making a lot less money than the other. One telecoms company might have the same number of subscribers as another, but the second company might be selling a much higher proportion of value-added services such as voicemail and data packages - here again, the financial value of one company would be higher than the other.

We think valuations based on operating metrics are a great way to get a rough grasp of where values *might* lie. They're easy to do, and the stats are usually readily available - it's not a secret how many rooms a hotel has, for instance. But you should always aim to use the other valuation methods as a check.

Another way of checking the numbers is simply to work out revenue and profit per room/subscriber. Do that for a number of comparable companies and you can easily see whether the business you're looking at is making financial returns above or below industry averages.

'Rules of Thumb'

Thomas L West's *Business Reference Guide* is a fantastic book if you want to value businesses, as all the work of generating sector averages has already been done for you. It sets out 'rules of thumb' for a huge number of sectors, using the revenues, asset and earnings based approaches we looked at earlier.

So for instance, if you're interested in buying a dental practice, the *Guide* suggests you should look at 30-50% of gross turnover, for goodwill, plus the value of the equipment, *or* 60% of gross turnover, net. As well as the rules of thumb, it gives some idea of how different types of business might rank, depending on their location and the type of clients using the practice.

Let's look at another sector - restaurants. The *Guide* suggests that restaurants should be valued at 30-35% of sales, or 2.5 to 4 x EBITDA. Of course, you'll need to look at location, rent (which should not be too high as a percentage of sales, of course, or it will be difficult to make a consistent profit), seasonality, conversion/refurbishment potential, and the state of the kitchen equipment and décor, before you decide which end of the range is the most appropriate value. And if you're selling, it will be the bottom end, If you trust the *Guide*, since it tells you that restaurants are currently a buyer's market - and the business might be worth more as real estate than as a business.

It goes into detail, too, about the characteristics of the sector and specific items you should look for in the accounts. If your background isn't finance, however well you think you know your business you may be surprised to find out about some of the misdeeds you can track down by a close reading of the financial statements! If you're buying into a sector that is relatively new to you, the *Guide* will really open your eyes with its recommendations on due diligence. For instance, it advises that if cost of goods is more than 35% of a restaurant's sales, somebody is skimming the stock.

The *Guide* is probably most useful for valuing average performers, rather than really high-performing businesses or turnarounds. It also tends to concentrate on the smaller business sectors most commonly bought or franchised by individuals. If you're interested in valuing a high tech business or a fairly large manufacturing business, the book is less useful.

Still, if reading this book has left you wanting to know even more about valuation, we'd heartily recommend the *Guide* as a step forward. Maybe you'll even end up in business as a business broker!

CHAPTER 8 – VALUING INTANGIBLE ASSETS

"This is the knowledge economy!"

That's a great thing to say, but there's one problem - how do you value knowledge? Fortunately, there are various techniques that can help you put a financial value on knowledge, as well as on other *intangible assets* such as brands, patents, and know-how.

There's still a lot of accounting controversy over intangibles and how (and whether) they can be represented in a balance sheet. Historically, goodwill has been seen as the difference between the asset value of a takeover target, and the price at which it was taken over. Goodwill was only ever recognised in the event of a takeover or disposal.

But for the purposes of company valuation, never mind what the accounting standards say - you're interested in finding out what a company's worth, not getting an audited statement. Since net book value is becoming less and less useful, we'll take a look at the intangibles that represent a much larger store of value for many companies today.

Imagine, for instance, Parker Pens. They have a huge share of the market for pens. They used to have a massive factory in Janesville, Wisconsin, and another in Newhaven, England. The net asset value included these factories and all the specialised equipment in them (including, apparently, big drums full of crushed walnut shells for polishing the gold nibs of fountain pens). Those factories were closed down, and now Parker manufactures its high end pens in France, and lower price point pens are made in China and through a licensing arrangement in India. So, what is Parker worth now? It doesn't have those big factory assets sitting on the balance sheet - but it *does* have a fantastic brand name. The value of the company is in that brand.

Many companies outsource production. They work on designing products, but they hire another company to do the manufacturing. Apple, for instance, doesn't manufacture the iPhone itself. It's the Apple brand, and Apple's design and programming skills, not the manufacturing, that creates the value.

Intangible assets split down into two categories, definite and indefinite. Definite assets relate to legal rights or contracts - for instance patents, domain names, copyrights, and royalty agreements. Indefinite intangibles are hazier - intellectual capital, brand names, trade secrets. You might consider customer lists, a firm's reputation, or particular manufacturing processes or technology protocols, to be intangible assets.

Let's look at some examples.

- A training company working with corporate clients might have few assets. It might be based in a rented office, and have a total twenty computers as its asset base, plus working capital. However, looking at its intangible assets, for a start, it will own the copyright of its training materials. It may have technology assets, such as a program for testing students at the end of a course, or distance learning software. It may let other training businesses use that software and charge a royalty.
- A life sciences company might not own all its own lab equipment; it might share facilities, and outsource much of the work. But it will have a lot of intangibles - drugs in testing, drug patents, possibly also a proprietary process for analysing genetic material.
- A Proptech company has created software and an internet platform for crowdsourcing real estate, in order to allow individual investors to place their capital into a number of rental properties. The technology and the network are likely to be worth a whole lot more than the servers they run on.

So how can we value these intangible assets? We need to look at their ability to generate a return for the business. Of course, you could argue that the earnings and DCF valuations you've done will already have recognised that - but sometimes, you may be looking at the purchase or sale of an intangible. For instance, you might want to buy the rights to a particular author's work. In that case you'd want a separate valuation. In the case of royalties or patents we probably have management accounting reports that help us to do this. For brands, there probably won't be any detailed financial statements - we'll have to make a few guesses as to what the brand value is.

Discounted cash flow and revenue based approaches are the most common to valuing intangible assets. Revenue is useful when you can't separate out the profitability of a brand from the rest of the business, because it's manufactured in the same facility as other products. You'll need to try to find comparable transactions to give you a steer on value - corporate acquisitions are more useful than stock market comparisons. Remember to add a discount for size - a mega-brand like Ben & Jerry's is worth more than a local ice cream maker's brand, however great the latter's ice cream might be.

Discounted cash flow, however, is the best way to look at intangible assets if you can identify both the revenue stream and the cost base.

Some technology assets (using the term quite broadly) can also be analysed on an avoided-cost basis - looking at what it would cost to buy the product from someone else or to build it yourself. For instance, if I buy a software platform for businesses to coordinate group purchases of office supplies, what would it cost to build it in-house? If I can buy a ready-made platform for that cost, I'm doing well because I'm buying something that's ready and working, instead of developing something that might not be ready within the next year.

But when you're looking at intangibles, you do need to keep your critical distance. As well as trying to put a quantitative value on them, think about what they're really worth.

- If you're looking at patents, can they be defended? Or are rip-off products already appearing, for instance, made in jurisdictions where intellectual property isn't well policed?
- Are trademarks in place for the brand you're looking at? If not, why not? Having a trademark in the US will not necessarily confer rights over the same name in Europe or Asia - check geographical coverage and don't make assumptions.
- How transferable is the value of intangibles? For instance, a restaurant with a celebrity chef might not be able to keep its Michelin stars or its value if she scoots off.
- Has the brand received investment and marketing support? Or has it been left to fend for itself?

Remember that the value of intangibles can change over time. Brands can lose market share, and technology and patents can be superseded by new, more efficient versions. Ensure your knowledge is fully up to date.

Antiquax is a well-known brand of wax designed specifically for the maintenance of antique furniture. It was part owned by Partridge Fine Arts, which went into administration; Intangible Business was then asked to value the brand.

Unfortunately, they found that it hadn't been invested in - possibly because of its owner's financial problems. Although it had a good reputation, it was poorly distributed - most retailers didn't carry the product, so customers who would have been interested in buying it were unable to find it, and purchased other brands instead. Some customers actually thought they didn't make it anymore! Investment would be needed to reinvigorate the brand and to improve the distribution network.

That investment had to be allowed for in the cash flow forecast. Attending exhibitions, creating new point-of-sale materials, and adding extra sales force isn't cheap. So despite the steady stream of revenue coming from the brand, and its good reputation, that depressed the current market value.

CHAPTER 9 – AN ART, NOT A SCIENCE

So far, we've been mainly looking at the numbers - different techniques of valuation and how to calculate the values. But once you've done the basic calculations, valuation stops being about the maths and becomes an art, rather than a science. If you have used each valuation method in turn, you probably have a range of valuations. Now you need to start to interpret them.

First of all, look at the variance between the highest and lowest. Look at how the values are distributed: are they clustered around the middle, or widely divergent? You may have one value that's an outlier, way out of sync with the others. That can tell you a lot about the business and about how confident you can be in your valuation.

- For instance, if all the valuations tend to cluster around a central point, and none are more than 10-15% away from the others, you can be pretty confident in your valuation. (That's unusual, as in most cases the asset-based valuation will be well below the others.)
- If you have a single outlier, is it the valuation that you might have expected to be very high (or low)? For instance, the net asset value of a technology business might be almost nothing. You might have expected the DCF valuation to come out higher than the others if you're looking at a business that has recently experienced poor profitability, but which you expect to turn around. You need to think through how confident you are in the divergent value - do you trust your forecasts enough to back the DCF valuation against the others? Or will you regard that as your potential upside, or as your margin of error, but try to secure the business at the lower valuation shown by your other results?
- If the *adjusted* book value is higher than the other values, that may be a warning to steer clear if you're interested in the business as a going concern. Suppose you want to buy a small hotel to manage, but it's worth more if you flatten it and sell the land off for housing.
- If all the values are very different, something's going on. Try to pinpoint any unusual factors - such as, for instance, the fact that the company is asset-rich but making a loss. But in this case, if we

couldn't work out why the valuations have all come out with very different totals, we'd have less confidence in the numbers.

Now it's probably time to go back and look at your notes from making the calculations. Were there particular assumptions you weren't particularly happy about? Are you sure your forecasts are robust? Look again at the comparison with other companies and consider the quality of the business you're valuing compared to the others. Now that you know which valuation methods that produced divergent numbers, go over them with a fine tooth comb - try to find anything you might have done that resulted in an atypical value. For instance, you may have put a really high discount rate into your DCF analysis but not discounted the PER and Price/EBITDA values, so the two methods are inconsistent.

Once you've done this second check you can look again at the range of values. Do you already have a gut feeling for whether you want to choose a lower, or a higher value? Do you have a gut feeling for which of the valuation methods is the most appropriate? That's good - write it down! The more you document the process, the easier it is to refer back to your notes during any negotiations and remind yourself *why* you set the values that you did.

Now, briefly recap the risks involved. Think about the business's strategy - how well equipped is it to handle future opportunities and threats? That might sound like corporate speak, but even a local bakery thinking about competition from supermarkets needs to have a strategy for competing - which might be an extended range of custom made cakes and desserts, high quality artisanal bread, a home delivery service, or long term contracts with canteens and retirement homes.

Think about any substantial single risks or negative industry trends. How much discount do you want to build into the valuation to take account of them? For instance, if you think there's a possibility that new regulations could increase the business's costs, or reduce its market (perhaps by introducing age verification for customers or making them put health warnings on products), you might want to discount the value according to how likely you think it is that the new regulations will be introduced.

You're looking for a range of values, not a single value. That may sound odd - after all, stock market analysts confidently say that a stock is “worth fifty bucks" and expect us to believe them. But actually, having a range of values is a real aid if you're aiming to buy or sell a business, because negotiations are going to be involved; if you have a range of values, you know what's the most you can probably ask from a purchaser, or what's the lowest offer you can make and not be shown the door - but you also have a feeling for where you might need to settle, or what's the absolute top price you can pay and still feel happy that you haven't overpaid.

CHAPTER 10 – WHAT TO LOOK FOR IN FINANCIAL STATEMENTS

We've covered all the basics of valuation already, but it's important also to look at the financial statements with a keen eye - and particularly at the notes to the accounts. This is stuff that your accountant will probably know backwards, but if you want to do business valuation properly, it doesn't hurt to have a feeling for the items that might be red flags, and to know where companies try to bury the bodies. Everything we've written in this chapter applies to all valuations, but it's particularly important for buyers.

For public companies that are listed on a stock exchange, you'll have extended data to look at. Even if you're not valuing that company, but using it as a comparison for the business you're looking at, it can be useful to read through the presentations to analysts (often on the website), and the discussion of operations at the front of the annual report. These may include additional industry-specific data, such as numbers of subscribers (for telecoms and pay-TV) or homes starts and completions (for housebuilders and developers), and can also sometimes flag up trends or new developments in the industry that you might have missed elsewhere.

Looking at the accounts is useless. Open a spreadsheet and start calculating the ratios. These will tell you far more about the business. There's a plethora of ratios you could use, but we'll highlight the ones that are most enlightening.

- Days Sales Outstanding (Receivables / sales x 365). You need to look at the historic and industry comparisons. Does it look as if the company is having trouble getting paid? An increase in DSO might reflect lax credit terms, failure to pursue bad debts, or poor creditworthiness of customers - or it might reflect one big customer going to the wall. If you have access to management accounts, ask for a receivables aging report so you can see how long customers are managing to extend their credit.
- Inventory days (inventory / cost of goods sold x 365). Is stock turning over as fast as you'd expect it to? If stock turnover has been slowing down, is the product failing to compete, or are there other reasons, such as poor distribution? Again, if you have access

to detailed figures, check to see exactly where the problem lies; a whole line of obsolete stock, or a downturn across the board? Remember to check for write-downs, which might temporarily make the position look better.

- Borrowings - look back in the notes to the accounts for the *maturity profile*. That will show you any debt that has to be repaid and how long the business has till it needs to repay it - if there's a big debt that comes due shortly, beware! (Though of course, that just might mean the business is available at a bargain price - and if you have the funds to pay off the debt, you'll have made a great purchase.)
- Look at the profit margins. You'll want to calculate gross margin (sales less cost of goods sold, as a percentage of sales) - this is particularly important for retailers, as it represents their direct costs - all other costs are fixed. If it's falling, it may indicate that the business can't pass on increased costs to its customers.
- EBITDA margin is probably the most useful single ratio you can calculate. Take the pre-tax operating profit, and add back interest, and then the depreciation and amortisation (you'll find that in the notes, most likely). Calculate this figure as a percentage of sales turnover. It takes out debt and tax, takes out depreciation because it's a non-cash item, and basically shows you the cash profitability of the business.
- Look at the return on assets. There are quite a few different ways to calculate this, that we won't go into here, but we particularly like to use EBITDA over total assets (that is, working capital plus fixed assets). It takes financing and tax out of the equation, and shows how efficiently the business is generating profit from the assets it holds - how much profit it's making for each dollar invested. The higher, the better, obviously!

When you're looking at the figures, you should also ask how that margin or return is being achieved. Are margins going up simply because the business is charging higher prices? That can boost returns for a while, but it might not be sustainable above a certain level, or customers will start to look elsewhere. Or does the business have a higher return on assets than comparable companies because it has a unique resource - a brewery that owns its own borehole for water, or a manufacturer that has designed its own high-specification production process for components and gained a cost advantage?

Sometimes being the dominant player in just one city can be a huge advantage. The local big player can afford to pay more for local advertising than national firms which don't have such a good foothold. Sometimes, local players pick off all the high margin business, leaving the big national firms, which are less nimble, to pick up the less profitable jobs. That's happened with parcels carriers and couriers, for instance.

Be suspicious if it looks as if cost cutting has boosted returns in the last couple of years. Cost cutting can also help increase margins in the short term, but eventually leaves the business with few options for margin growth - and sometimes with a less competitive product and a less motivated workforce.

Look out for changes in accounting practice. For instance, depreciation rates can be changed in order to charge less depreciation and thereby boost the operating profit figure.

One item you should always look for is related party transactions. Sales to associate companies, loans to directors, or purchases of shares in companies that are also significant customers, are all warning signs unless they can be properly explained to your satisfaction. (Loans to directors in smaller businesses are sometimes simply driven by tax efficiency.)

The relationship with the auditors is also worth watching. If a company has changed auditors once, that might be because they experienced poor customer service, or found another auditor would charge them significantly less for the same job. But if a company changes auditors twice within a few years, there might be a bit of a problem. Another thing to watch out for is a company that uses the same accountants as auditors, consultants, and to manage payroll and other functions - how independent is that audit going to be?

And look for sharp accounting practices. Despite tight audit requirements, there are still quite a few areas where companies can pick and choose their treatment of items. One we really hate is capitalisation of current costs. Normally, if you spend money wining and dining a customer, or leafleting potential customers, or buying TV ads, or pitching for business, that comes out of your current costs - it comes out of profit and loss account. But some cable TV companies decided their figures would look a whole lot better if they treated this as an investment, instead. The costs were put on the balance sheet as an asset, and so profits increased by the amount that *wasn't* written off. Many software companies, with rather more reason, capitalise some of their research and development costs.

Be very careful if you see this going on. It's not *wrong* necessarily, but it's not the most conservative way of treating costs - and it also means the net book value has been inflated.

CHAPTER 11 – BUYING OR SELLING A BUSINESS

SELLING

If you're selling a business, one of the things you need to think about is timing. Remember that there are stock market booms and stock market busts, and that valuations change because of the market's movements, but also because of changes in competitive conditions.

You may also have your own timing to think about; when to make the transition to the next generation of a family firm, when to retire. It's important not to miss the boat - if you wait five years to sell, but the industry is no longer looking as optimistic as it did at the start, you might actually get less for the business the longer you hold on.

Don't miss the boat. An expert witness on valuation remembers a divorce case that happened about the time of the tech market crash. The main asset in dispute, on which the witness had been asked to deliver a valuation, was a VPN company that the husband had set up and developed into a major provider. It started at a value of about $50m, but the wife kept challenging the husband's figures. By the time the couple got their divorce, the value of the business was down to just $2m.

Another cautionary tale also comes from the tech sector. Myspace sold out to News Corporation in 2005, when it was the biggest social networking site in the world. It was valued at $580m. But by 2008, it had been overtaken by Facebook. In June 2011, News Corp sold it - for just $35m.

Coming right down to local level, even though valuations might not see the kind of dramatic swings that the tech sector has seen over the last two decades, you can't take a successful sale as a given - particularly if buyers depend on bank finance. A bookshop owner with a huge stock of second-hand books wanted to retire. Five years before, he'd had a good offer for the shop with all the stock and the living quarters above. He didn't take it. Now, he found no one was interested in the business. One or two people made enquiries, but couldn't raise enough finances to take the business over. The shop was worth more if he sold it for conversion to a house. He got his retirement fund, and in addition was able to warehouse the stock and trade on the internet. But he had always wanted to pass the shop on as a going concern, and was sad that he wasn't able to.

So if you're aiming to sell a business, start the process early. For instance, start getting your documentation in order. Tighten up the book-keeping and if you want to sell a part of the business, start producing separate financial accounts for it. Clean up any 'dirty laundry' - make write-offs on obsolete stock, for instance.

Deals take time. Even selling an apartment can take several months; businesses are more difficult to sell and can take over a year. Buyers will normally want to do their due diligence, or to send their accountant to do it; if you don't have the numbers they want, it could take extra time to produce the right information. You may have two or three potential buyers. Negotiating the price takes time.

Get started well before you need to sell. If you want to retire in five years' time, it's not too early to start thinking about what the business is worth, what could make it worth more, and what could help make a quick and orderly sale.

If you find a buyer, you need to do *your* due diligence by assessing their ability to pay. Are they spending cash, or depending on a bank loan? Have they started talking to their bank, or will you need to allow time for them to do so? How sure are they that they'll get their finance - do they have personal assets that they'll use as collateral? Buyers who bridle at this kind of questioning may just be prickly - but equally, they could have something to hide.

Make very, very sure that you do your due diligence if the buyer wants to issue promissory notes or give you shares at part of the deal. And if you get shares, beware of lock-in periods and other restrictions on sale.

BUYING

As a business buyer you'll need to do due diligence, or, in more vulgar parlance, 'kick the tyres'. Quite a lot of it is about checking that the numbers in the accounts are real - adding a quality assessment to the quantities shown.

Here are just a few of the ways you might do your due diligence.

- Spot-checking customers. Talk to customers and ask them when they first bought from the company. If there don't seem to be any new customers in the last five years, beware! Equally, if the company's been going for ten years but none of the customers you speak to have dealt with it for more than six months, is there something going wrong that you should know about? Also ask customers what other suppliers they use, and try to get a feeling for how easily they could move their business if they wanted to.

- Checking stocks. A physical inventory audit will turn up signs of obsolescence, or of slow moving, older stock. Are stationery cupboards full of old posters and unused marketing materials? Are there heaps of cardboard boxes in the back of a loading bay? Keep an eye open for any signs of theft or 'skimming'. See if you can work out what's being paid for stock and if it's normal for the industry - buying too dear and selling too cheap is a sure way to disaster, but more importantly, some hotel bar managers have been known to cut a deal with their suppliers. They pay 150% of the market price for all their spirits, and pocket half of that themselves while the supplier still gets an inflated price.
- Checking the plant and equipment. Is it kept in good order? Has it been well maintained? Is it in use? If you see plant that's mothballed, or that's not working when you visit, find out why.

I often get asked how you can judge the state of equipment if you're not an industry specialist. It's not that difficult, though. A meeting of bank staff a few years ago turned up some wonderful stories of 'the worst plant I ever visited'.

One junior banker was on a tour of a small specialised foundry. All the furnaces were lit, and the workers were clearly busy, from the amount of noise they were making. This guy needed to use the bathroom, and took a break from the tour. On his way back to rejoin the group, he noticed most of the furnaces were dying down, and the workers had all disappeared. There was, he told his boss, definitely something wrong with the accounts.

That's nothing, another investment officer said. She'd visited a factory where the overhead conveyor kept dropping product on the floor because the grippers didn't operate properly. Fortunately, no one actually got hit by falling glass , but when she added up the accidents she'd seen, she reckoned that a quarter to a third of the product never reached the end of the production line. No wonder costs were the highest in the industry!

But a third guy had the best of all stories. He visited a business that was supposed to be making precision instrumentation. True, it did have a few micrometers and dial indicators on show, but it turned out it made most of its money making kids' toys,

Keep your eyes open and your wits about you, and above all, do the legwork - and you'll be protecting yourself against business disasters like these.

Take a good look at the products and where they are in the product lifecycle: are they developing, or are they mature or declining? Will they need marketing investment to kick-start them? A good example here is the craft beer movement. Beers from the first wave of craft breweries became 'old news' as new styles like sours and 'juicy hazy IPAs' arrived, and some of those first wave breweries have now ceased trading.

- If it's relevant, look at the research pipeline. What new products does the business have coming along? If there's nothing new on the horizon, in a tech or fashion dependent industry, that could be bad news.
- Check if a business has had any insurance refused. That's a big red flag. Many retailers that have hit the skids were first refused trade credit insurance.
- Check contracts with suppliers. Are supplies secure? How much can suppliers increase prices? Check rent agreements - can the rental be increased? How does it compare with other similar property?
- Check service agreements with customers and most importantly, in any service business which has formal service agreements, check if there have been any breaches and how much that has cost. How large a penalty will the company pay if it can't keep on track of major projects?
- Check the payroll. Does it all add up to the number in the accounts? Are employees getting paid market rates? Less, and you could have a problem recruiting - more, and someone's feather-bedding.
- Check the sales turnover against real world common sense. You can even 'go undercover', or have someone do it for you. One

junior equity analyst camped out for the day in a cafe opposite a factory gate to count trucks going in and coming out. His day netted him a fat bonus - he'd worked out there was no way the factory was making the numbers that the boss had said it would.

- Check title (Does the business actually own its premises, or rent? Do the same with intellectual property.)
- Check zoning / land use / planning permissions, and any environmental regulations that could increase business costs. Never trust a business owner to tell you all of this - he may not know! Many small production businesses get started as an artisan working in a garage - when the business grows, it stays in the garage, and hey, isn't that against the regulations? That might have worked okay for the original owner, but you should be very careful about investing money in this situation.
- Check for any pending lawsuits. Litigation can destroy a business's value. (It could also mean you are better off simply buying the business assets, rather than buying the business.)
- Take a look at similar businesses in the local area, if relevant - are there more starting up, or closing?

Sometimes the decision on whether to buy a business is a very personal one. A small tech company was for sale at what looked quite a bargain price, but two things niggled. One was that the chief technology officer somehow never seemed to be available for a meeting. The other was that the CEO really didn't seem switched on to technology; he needed to ask his secretary to print out his e-mails and couldn't use the remote control on a video.

But even so, the deal didn't actually die until the CEO, when asked about projections for the total share of his business, said "Guys, this will be bigger than the internet. We are actually going to replace the internet."

If the owner of a business looks like a fantasist, or seems to have missed a trick - like a fashion brand that has no social media policy - then you should be worried.

CONCLUSION

However complicated financial analysts and consultants make it look, business valuation formulas are simple enough for any business owner who has enough mathematical smarts to prepare accounts or price a product to be able to handle. It's difficult to overemphasise how useful a grasp of valuation can be.

A seat of your pants quick valuation can be very useful. You might want to assess whether a competing business is within your reach as a takeover target, or whether a demerger makes sense, before you spend time and money on going any further. You might just want to see whether your idea of making your business into your retirement pension will actually work, or whether the sale proceeds would only support a somewhat diminished lifestyle.

More advanced techniques, perhaps with professional assistance, come into play if you're serious. And if you ever get to the stage when you're preparing an IPO, of course, you'll have to have a lot of professional help - and pay handsomely for it.

If you're involved in buying or selling a business, a good grasp of valuation will help immensely when it comes to negotiating the price, because you'll really understand what goes into the valuation, and you'll have a better feel for what is a bit of a stretch, and what's way too far.

Knowing how to value a business can also help you to run your own investments. Stock market analysis has exactly the same basic tools as business valuation, and while you might not want to try to beat Warren Buffett at his own game, knowing the basics can help you avoid bad personal investments such as over-hyped IPOs.

Some people would take it even further. Every time you evaluate a major business decision, you should look at what it might do to your business valuation. Will it improve the long term value of the business - not just revenues, or profitability in the short term? Building a business is about building value - and if you understand both business and valuation, you'll be able to do both.

Resources / sources of information

Financial data for publicly quoted companies can be found on their own websites, and on stock exchange sites (Nasdaq.com, nyse.com). A quicker way to access the most important financial statistics is to use a finance portal like Yahoo (finance.yahoo.com) or Marketwatch, which also gives share prices and analyst forecasts.

Analysing an industry? Trade journals are a good place to look, but remember they will always tend to have an upbeat bias in their articles, as they have advertisers who will be upset by a negative vibe. For instance, real estate magazines are never going to be the first to carry articles on a property market collapse or over-extended mortgage multiples. It's also worth searching investment paper and magazine sites like Barron's and the Wall Street Journal - some articles will be too heavily investment-focused, but there's some insightful analysis of industry trends, particularly in Barron's roundtable discussions. Some accountancy firms also publish analyses of industry sectors. But the source that a lot of business people miss out is research published by credit insurers such as Euler Hermes, Atradius and Coface. It can be highly informative and it's based on hard fact, not hype.

For analysing local markets, start with local papers - and don't forget, adverts placed by local businesses are as informative as the editorial. Many local papers have a regular business section. Don't just check for the business involved, or its peers, though, as there's a lot more useful information in the local paper: local government's planning strategies, population growth and demographics, and even local banking trends, all of which might be useful to know.

Industry average costs of capital and other data are shown by an academic economist at Stern School of Business, New York University

(http://pages.stern.nyu.edu/~adamodar/New_Home_Page/home.htm).

Aswath Damodaran teaches corporate finance and valuation, and provides an annual update of a huge database, and several monthly data series. It may not sound sexy, but it's a really great source of information.

If you enjoyed this book, can you please leave a review for it?

Click here to leave a review for this book on Amazon

Thanks for your support!

www.ingramcontent.com/pod-product-compliance
Lightning Source LLC
LaVergne TN
LVHW022316200926
848481LV00004B/1365
9781807650292